THEY DIED TOO YOUNG

BOB MARLEY

BY
Millie Gilfoyle

D1327008

This edition first published by Parragon Books Ltd in 1995

Produced by
Magpie Books Ltd, London

Copyright © Paragon Book service Ltd 1995
Unit 13–17, Avonbridge Trading Estate, Atlantic Road
Avonmouth, Bristol, BS11 9QD

Illustrations courtesy of: Rex Features.

ISBN 0 75251 115 7

A copy of the British Library Cataloguing in Publication
Data is available from the British Library.

Typeset by Hewer Text Composition Services, Edinburgh
Printed in Singapore by Printlink International Co.

COUNTRY BOY

'Auntie Ciddy, Auntie Ciddy!' Mrs Hanson bustled into her local grocery shop, flustered and excited. Just the day before, she said, Ciddy's son had read her palm, describing tiny details of her life and foretelling events which had come true already. Ciddy paid little attention – until the local policeman, a noted sceptic, said he too had been amazed by the boy's fortune-telling.

It was Jamaica, 1950. The boy, Robert Nesta Marley, was just five years old, and growing up in a culture full of 'duppies' (spirits) and 'obeah' (witchcraft). He lived with his mother in the tiny village of Nine Miles, in St Ann, the beautiful 'garden parish' of Jamaica, with its sandy beaches, lush hills and rich crops of bananas, coffee and coconuts.

When Bob Marley's parents met, his mother Cedella (Ciddy) was just eighteen, the sixth of nine children from a family of peasant farmers. His father, Captain Norval Sinclair Marley, was a fifty-year-old white Jamaican from a 'respectable' family, active in business. Norval himself was in the army. Their romance was secret, and when Cedella discovered she was pregnant, she was both proud and terrified. She knew her

father, Omeriah Malcolm, would disap-
prove strongly even though Norval had
promised to marry her and to support the
child.

When Omeriah Malcolm found out he
exploded with fury. Cedella even tried to
run away, but after a long and heated
argument the two men resolved their
differences and a wedding date was set.
Then gossip about the impending marriage
reached the Marleys, and in their horror
they denounced and disinherited Norval.

The couple were married in June 1944;
then, the day after the wedding, Norval
left. He told his bride he was leaving to
take up a new job, in Kingston, as he could
now scarcely afford to support himself, let
alone a family. He promised to visit often,

but came back only twice during her pregnancy.

Bob Marley – 'Nesta' as he was known when young – was born on 6 February 1945, a light-skinned baby with the thin lips and straight nose of his father. Norval visited occasionally, and sent some money, but the visits became increasingly rare. To make ends meet, Cedella's father helped her set up a tiny grocery shop, selling farm produce, in the hamlet of Alva near Nine Miles. It was a tight-knit rural community made up of a dozen or so closely related families, and as Nesta grew up he helped in the shop and on the farm, looking after his grandfather's goats. With Norval absent, Omeriah Malcolm was a strong influence: he was an ambitious and successful farmer, but also widely respected as a herbalist and 'myalman', who had learned the secrets of healing and of fighting 'obeah', from his 'myalman' father.

Jamaicans' belief in the supernatural is strongly rooted in history. Jamaica was originally populated by Arawak Indians, but after Christopher Columbus landed there in 1495, the Spanish, and later the British, shipped in African slaves to work in the sugar and banana plantations. In time, influences from Europe and Africa fused into a complex culture mixing Christianity with faith in 'myalmen' and fear of spirits such as the child-stealing 'blackheart mon'. Slavery on the island was abolished in 1834, but even freedom made little difference: the injustice and oppression suffered by the slaves was still keenly felt by many of their descendants.

Nesta Marley had in some ways an enviable childhood, growing up in rural St Ann with its abundance and its relaxed, 'soon come' philosophy. According to his mother, Nesta was a bright child, with an unnervingly direct gaze which even she sometimes found intimidating. When he was four, Cedella enrolled him at the local school. He did very well, and a year later his father wrote suggesting that he would get a better education in Kingston. Omeriah agreed with the scheme and arrangements were made for Nesta to stay with relations in Kingston, with his father living nearby.

Cedella broke the news the day he was due to go. Nesta shrieked and wept, but the plan was fixed, and he was taken to town in his best clothes to catch the 'bungo-bungo' (country bumpkin) bus to Kingston. Cedella realized he'd never seen a car before, as, saying goodbye, she placed him in the care of an elderly cousin, a 'higgler' (pedlar) on her weekly run to market. It was a long journey, and when the bus started to crawl through the narrow streets of Kingston, passing seas of faces, handcarts, and mounds of rubbish, Nesta burst into tears. At the bus depot, he was handed over to another stranger, an elderly white man in a soldier's uniform, who drove him away on a donkey cart.

It was almost a month before Cedella discovered her son was missing. The relations in Kingston wrote asking why he hadn't arrived, and when she tried to contact Norval, she found that no-one knew where he was. Father and son had completely disappeared – and the worst part was there seemed no way of finding either of them.

Cedella fell ill, and the family spent much of their time casting spells and praying for guidance. The breakthrough came in August 1951, more than a year later. Maggie, a higgler friend of Cedella's, ran into her shop one day, shouting out that she'd seen Nesta. The day before, she and her niece had been in Kingston, and Nesta had called out to them, asking why his mother hadn't been to see him. Maggie couldn't remember the address, but her niece was sure it was Heywood Street, and they set off to find him. They searched for a long time, but the street seemed strangely deserted, and Cedella started to get frantic. Then, an old man pointed out her son: a tubby child in clothes full of holes, playing football in an alley.

It turned out that Nesta had been living with an elderly woman named Miss Grey. She was frail and ill, clearly in no state to look after a six-year-old. She hadn't seen Captain Marley since he had brought Nesta to live there and she had had no idea how to contact the rest of the boy's family.

Once home, there was much celebrating, with the villagers blaming the whole episode on the evils of the city. Daily life was much as before, except that Nesta refused to read palms, saying he was now a singer. He used to drum on the vegetable bins in his mother's shop, sing-

ing songs he'd learned in Kingston:
'Please, Mister, won't ya touch me toma-
to! Touch me yam, me pumpkin an'
potato!'

A year passed, then Cedella started to feel
restless. She determined to move to Kingston, and, encouraged by her boyfriend,
Toddy Livingston, ventured to tell her
father. She could earn more in the city,
she argued, and in time maybe save
enough to move to America. Omeriah
eventually gave his consent, though he
suggested that Nesta, his favourite grand-
son, stay in the country for a few years.

So, when his mother went to live in
Kingston, Nesta was left in Nine Miles.
Cedella planned to move to her brother
Solomon's house when he left for Eng-

land, but meanwhile, she and Toddy took rooms off the rum bar where Toddy worked. Cedella cooked in restaurants, and worked as a laundress and house-keeper for various rich households up-town, sometimes going back to Nine Miles at weekends, but more often stay-ing in the city.

Nesta had been increasingly independent and naughty since his time in Kingston and after a while he proved too much for his grandfather to cope with. Recognizing this, Omeriah sent both Nesta and his cousin Slegger to live with Cedella's sister Amy, renowned for her strictness with children. The arrangement worked well for months, with Amy glad of the extra help, and the boys respecting their aunt's discipline. Then, one Sunday, Amy

Bob Marley

The coast at St Ann, Jamaica

decided to leave the boys in charge of the afternoon meal while she went to church. The meal was the traditional Sunday treat for the whole family, rice and peas (kidney beans) cooked in coconut milk – and leaving the boys to cook it was a tribute to their trustworthiness – and a way of showing off her iron control. Unfortunately, the plan backfired: Nesta and Slegger ate most of the food themselves, and, taking the rest of it with them, ran back to Omeriah's. Amy, publicly humiliated, was furious, and refused to take the boys back. Omeriah saw it was time for Nesta to be reunited with his mother.

TRENCH TOWN

Nesta's return to Kingston was softened slightly by the presence of Bunny Livingston, Toddy's son. Nesta was ten now, Bunny less than two years younger, and they soon became firm friends, part of a companionable makeshift family. The large ghetto schools had bad reputations and were said to foster delinquency, so Nesta was sent to the Model Private School. Thanks to his earlier spell in Kingston, his new life came as no great shock, though he was now much more aware of the turbulence around him — poverty, deprivation and violence.

Around this time, Cedella learned from a relation that Captain Marley had resurfaced in Kingston, and remarried, bigamously. She took him to court, then, a few months later, learned that he had died of a heart attack.

When Cedella's brother Solomon finally moved to England, Cedella was overjoyed. Now they could move to his house, in one of the 'government yards' in Trench Town. These yards were built to meet the housing shortage after the hurricanes in 1944 and 1951, so the buildings were relatively new, and sturdy, with kitchens and indoor lavatories.

They lacked the community spirit of the old tenant yards, where people cooked outdoors in the Jamaican tradition, but the rent would be cheap and the yards were a step up from their current accommodation.

Trench Town, though, was a rough area, originally built over a sewage drain. When they arrived, a donkey cart laden with their possessions, they found their new home behind a high concrete wall, one of twelve apartments surrounded by squatters' hovels. People stared and skinny hens ran around the yard. The ground was littered with dead cockroaches, and there was little greenery in sight. Outside the government yards, running water was virtually unknown, and the slum dwellers had to dig latrines. The areas nearby were similar, Boy's Town, Lizard City and Concrete Jungle, while the scavengers, the very lowest in the ghetto hierarchy, lived on a rubbish dump known as the Dungle.

Nesta and Bunny found Trench Town tough at first and couldn't understand why they had moved there. It was a time of great social and political unrest. On the street, most boys were looked on as potential hoodlums, and many gradually grew into 'rude boys' – bitter, violent teenagers who despised authority, and were often mixed up in robberies and ratchet (blade) fights. Teenage girls were confused, harassed by their families if they mixed with boys, yet rejected as 'mules' (barren and useless) if they hadn't had a child by the age of 17.

In time, Nesta grew accustomed to his new surroundings, and found he loved the sense of belonging. He learned to play cards and dominoes, became skilled at football, learned how to fight – and was soon 't'rowing partner' (swearing) as well as the next boy. Jamaica's first radio station had started in 1950, and in 1959 came another one which played records by local artists. A neighbour in the government yard had a radio which hung from a clothes-line and Nesta and Bunny would spend whole evenings transfixed – especially by the blues and R & B from America.

At fourteen it was time for Nesta to leave school. Cedella and Toddy decided he should be apprenticed to a welder, but Nesta himself was not keen: it was badly paid work, dangerous and dirty – and he'd be teased, as 'welder' was street slang for 'stud'. That didn't really matter though, as he already had quite a reputation as a street fighter, and, much to his mother's horror, had won the friendship and respect of the local 'rude boys'.

Nesta agreed to the apprenticeship for his mother's sake, but he had ambitions of his own. It was common knowledge that the only paths to success from the ghettos were through crime, sport or music, and Nesta long ago decided to be a singer. For a while now he and Bunny had been practising in the yard, with Bunny playing along on his 'guitar' – a large sardine can strung with electrical wire.

They had also started going to the 'blues dances' held at various outdoor venues around Kingston: it was here that all the new music — including ska — was played. The DJs all had exaggerated names: 'Count Machuki', 'King Sporty', and 'Sir Coxsone Downbeat', the last famous for his 'control tower' of turntables and the way he 'supplied da beat to feed da heat!' In the mid-to-late 1950s the competition between the 'Sound Systems' was almost a war. Spies went to rival dances to watch what got the best response, and it was common practice to scratch labels off new records to confound the spies. Some employed 'dance crashers' to rubbish their rivals' music, loudly criticize the DJs or even to provoke violence among the dancers.

Two of the Sound System leaders, Duke Reid and Sir Coxsone Dodd, emerged as clear winners in the battle, and in 1959 Sir

Bob lived in the Trench Town area of Kingston

Early encouragement came from
Desmond Dekker

Coxsone set up his own recording studios, recognizing the money to be made from Jamaican music. Nesta, and all the other would-be stars, spent hours there every day, listening to the music pumping out from above the door. By 1962, Nesta had written a few songs, and, encouraged by Desmond Dekker, a local boy who had already made a record, he decided to approach Coxsone Dodd. When he turned up, Dodd was nowhere to be found. Instead Nesta ran into Leslie Kong, a Chinese Jamaican who ran a restaurant/record shop/ice cream parlour, and who had recently branched into the music business. He was with a 14-year-old, who told Nesta he'd taken the stage name Jimmy Cliff and that Leslie Kong had just produced his song 'Dearest Beverley'.

Kong ordered Nesta to sing then and there, laughing when he said he had no guitar. Nesta was angry and nervous, but sang 'Judge Not', a song he'd written inspired by his grandfather. Kong asked him in and they went through to a dimly lit room. Recording equipment was stacked up inside, and a few musicians sat around: within an hour two songs had been recorded. Nesta got £20, and a few hours later was hurrying home with two black vinyl discs – his recording career had begun!

Later he realized he didn't know anyone who owned a record player, and that the label on 'Judge Not' proclaimed 'By Bob Morley'. Still, his song was on the jukebox of a nearby rum shop, and he spent much of his spare time selecting his song and watching the reaction of passers by. In the end, the owner of the rum shop had enough and removed it from the jukebox.

Now seventeen, Nesta had served his apprenticeship and was employed by a master welder. He was working as usual one day, daydreaming as he repaired a bicycle, when suddenly he screamed, dropping his acetylene torch: some shards of hot metal had pierced his eye. The boss swore: he provided goggles but no-one bothered to wear them. Nesta was in agony. His mother put him to bed, tied 'strong man's weed' to his forehead, and boiled up rum broth. The next day she took him to hospital, where a doctor spent several hours trying to pull out the slivers – without success, and without anaesthetic. The doctor succeeded in the end, but it was a long and painful process. Home again, and fully recovered, Bob – as he now preferred to be known – made his mother promise not to make him return to welding. Instead, he would be a full-time singer.

TASTING SUCCESS

Soon after 'Judge Not' came out, Cedella and Bob had taken a bus to Montego Bay at the far end of the island, to attend a big talent show. Bob got up on stage and sang his song, and was overwhelmed by the applause that followed: it was a good feeling.

The successful singing duo Higgs and Wilson had been 'discovered' at just such a talent contest, and their resulting single sold more than 30,000 copies. Joe Higgs was also well known as one of the first Rastafarian musicians targeted by the police. In 1930 when Haile Selassie was crowned Emperor of Ethiopia, Rastas hailed him as Jah (God), and Rastas' beliefs are based on honouring him and on the idea that black people can only escape oppression by returning to Africa. These beliefs, combined with the Rasta 'dreadlocks' and the sacrament of smoking 'herb' (marijuana), meant that in the early 1960s most Rastafarians were social outcasts or hermits. (The more 'acceptable' aspects, such as observing strict 'ital' dietary laws and reading the Bible, made less of an impact!)

Joe Higgs was different. He was a Rastafarian, but unusual in that he commanded

Hailie Selassie visited Jamaica in 1966

Peter Tosh

respect from all quarters, including the 'rudies'. In 1959 he had been set up by the police, beaten and imprisoned, but he retained his dignity, and once freed, gently discouraged the rude boys' calls for vengeance. Having attracted all this attention, Higgs decided to focus it – and began to hold free music sessions at his home in Trench Town. A professional, and a perfectionist, he taught music theory, the techniques of breath control and harmony.

Bob Marley had continued to write songs with Bunny in addition to his solo efforts, and now they'd joined forces with another youth, Peter McIntosh. The three of them started going along to Higgs's workshops, and Higgs singled out Bob for special attention: he was particularly struck by his voice. Boosted by this, Bob insisted that the trio should be more professional, and as a first step, Peter Tosh (his new stage name) managed to persuade a local vicar to lend him a guitar, long-term.

Peter was a tall, arrogant boy who boasted to friends about his musical talents. Abandoned by his parents, and with no trade to help him, music was his passport to a better life, and often he took it much too seriously. He also liked to say he was leader of the band. Actually, there was no leader, though Bob was the only one with experience. He now had five more recordings behind him, one of which, 'One Cup of Coffee', had made quite an impact. This, combined with Joe Higgs's encouragement, gave Bob extra confidence and he began to radiate a calm assurance which unnerved many he worked with.

Bob broke off his arrangement with Leslie Kong, after Kong refused to pay him. Rumours went round that when the producer withheld the money, Bob had pointed at him and made an odd prediction: they would work together again, he said, and Kong would make lots of money from it – but would never enjoy the money.

Around this time, the band – originally The Teenagers, renamed The Wailers – acquired some extra members. Junior Braithwaite now shared lead vocals, while Cherry Green and Beverly Kelso joined as backing singers. They practised together for weeks before approaching Joe

Higgs. He recognized their commitment and potential, and started to coach them seriously, advising Bob to sing whenever he could to help strengthen his voice.

They worked hard and before long Joe Higgs made arrangements for The Wailers to audition with Coxsone Dodd. Dodd's Sound System and record business had continued to prosper, and he'd just set up his own one-track studio. The Wailers auditioned one Sunday, and Dodd offered them a contract straight away: he would pay £20 for each side recorded, and would reserve the exclusive right both to release their records and to act as their manager. They agreed.

The Wailers were very nervous at the first recording session but they managed to record two ska tracks, and when one of these began to catch on at his Sound System, Clement Dodd called them back for more recording. By this time Junior Braithwaite had left as he was about to move to America, and Cherry had been dropped as too unprofessional. This annoyed Dodd, who complained that they had to organize themselves, and told them they needed a lead singer.

After some discussion it was decided that Bob should lead for the time being, as 'Simmer Down', their best song of the moment, was one of his. Dodd liked the song too, and this time shipped in some of his top session musicians for the recording. It was a raw, powerful song and, most unusually, dealt with the raging problem of street crime – speaking directly to the rude boys in the language they used themselves. It was certainly topical: Dodd himself had started carrying a gun for protection, and the approach was quite new, music rooted in the ghetto and directed at fellow 'sufferahs'.

'Simmer Down' was a smash hit, reaching number 1 in February 1964.

Clement Dodd now faced a dilemma: whether to encourage The Wailers' individual style, or follow his original plan and groom them into a slick R & B group. Unsure what to do, he arranged for them to compete at a talent show at the Majestic Theatre. He gave them an advance against royalties to cover the stage outfits he'd chosen: a sequinned dress for Beverly, pointy shoes and a gold lamé suit for

each of the boys. He also initiated a
weekly salary of £3.00 each.

In an attempt to please as many people as
possible, he got The Wailers to sing a
combination of popular Motown and
R & B numbers and their own 'ghetto
songs'. They were a huge success, and the
audience loved them, though they lost the
contest – narrowly – to The Uniques. Bob
was incensed, convinced The Wailers
were the better band. He started a fight
backstage with the winners, and the police
were called. This episode made Dodd
nervous, but it didn't harm the band's
reputation: word simply spread that The
Wailers were not to be messed with.

In her own way, Cedella was just as single-
minded as her son. She had been writing

to friends in Delaware for years, and eventually decided to see for herself what America was like. She liked what she saw. Discovering that she was carrying Toddy's child settled the matter: Toddy was amenable to her leaving, the thought of raising another child in Trench Town did not appeal, and Bob was now nineteen and making his own way. She found it hard to understand her son's attachment to Kingston – the place frightened her – but she saw his determination, and recognized how important his music was to him. Soon after Pearl was born, Cedella and the baby left for America.

It was a busy time for The Wailers, with lots of live shows and new records, many of which became hits. One day, they were taking their usual short cut to the recording studio, when they were accosted by a pretty teenager. She introduced herself as Rita Anderson, and explained that she knew they were The Wailers, and she'd often seen them from her house nearby. Peter flirted, and the others virtually ignored her, but after that they often met her, and a friendship began to grow. Unknown to The Wailers, Rita was in a group of her own, The Soulettes, which consisted of Rita, her friend Precious, and her cousin Dream. Dream had also struck up an acquaintance with the band, and through them managed to set up a meeting with Coxone Dodd.

The Wailers were surprised when Rita appeared at the studio, but The Soulettes' audition was successful, and Dodd chose Bob to coach them. As The

Soulettes became familiar faces at the studio, Peter's flirting continued. In contrast Bob was impatient and irritable, and Rita's band resented his harsh criticisms and general attitude.

One day Bunny brought Rita a note from Bob. When she saw it was a love letter she was angry, assuming he must be making fun of her. It seemed she was wrong, though, as more notes appeared. Bob still said nothing, and was as strict as ever in rehearsals. Confused, Rita decided to confront him. One evening she went round to the room off the studios where he'd been living since Cedella left. Despite his success, he was not living in style: the room was tiny, with just enough space for a crude bed (an old door plus straw mattress) and a small table. The table

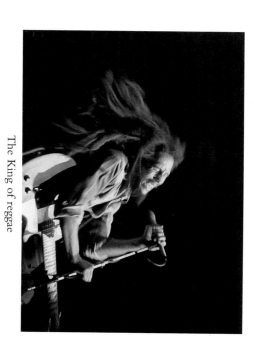

The King of reggae

The Wailers in the recording studio

was piled with letters, and when Rita
exclaimed at these, Bob told her they
were all from his mother, who was worry-
ing about him.

Rita asked him about the love notes, but
he wouldn't reply, and she burst into tears.
Bob calmed her and they sat and talked.
While they were talking, Bob admitted
that he'd been too immersed in his music
to reply to his mother, and asked Rita if
she would write on his behalf. She agreed,
seeing a way of finding out more about
this strange character. The next day she
came round to show him the letter, but he
told her instead how he was being plagued
by duppies (spirits) during the night. Rita,
a regular church-goer, said she didn't
believe in duppies – but, as Bob seemed
genuinely distressed, she agreed to stay in

his room that night to witness whatever happened.

The story goes that in the middle of the night she woke to find herself lying in the middle of the floor, sweating and shivering, and gripped by an all-consuming terror. She tried to scream but no sound came, and she felt as if she was being held down. Eventually she managed to move enough to wake Bob, and was then violently sick. Bob comforted her; he was not surprised, as this had been happening to him every night. No wonder he was tired and irritable in the studios!

They agreed that Bob must find somewhere else to live. Since Cedella left, Toddy hadn't been able to afford the government yard, and had had to move, so Bob was on his own. Rita suggested he could stay with her, at least for a few days. Her parents had moved to England when she was eight, leaving their children with relations, and Rita lived with a strict aunt. The situation was far from ideal: the house was small and crowded, and since Rita had become pregnant accidentally the year before, the aunt had been stricter than ever. Rita shared a bed with her cousin, and Sharon – her baby – had a cot in the same room. Bob would have to wait until they were all asleep, then climb in through the window and slip out before daybreak. It was that or the streets, so Bob agreed.

Unfortunately the baby started crying in the night, and Rita's aunt came in to find Bob disappearing through the bedroom window. Furious, shrieking with rage, she pushed Rita through the window after him, and the young couple spent the night huddling outside, trying to decide what to do. The next day Rita steeled herself to face her aunt. She said that she and Bob had been sleeping, not having sex, and that in any case they were in love: Bob might well become a father to Sharon. The aunt was eventually convinced, and she grudgingly agreed to let them live in the shed behind her house. So they moved in, and Bob, no longer plagued by duppies, once more immersed himself in his music.

That September, 1964, Bob had a strange dream: that a new house was being built in place of his grandfather Omeriah's. Two days later, news came that Omeriah was dead. The family gathered in Nine Miles

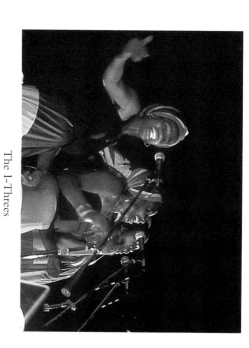

The I-Threes

'a happy rhythm with a sad sound with a good vibration'

for the traditional nine days of receiving mourners, cleaning and polishing, story-telling and casting spells to honour the dead and protect the living. Omeriah had made it plain he wanted Bob to inherit his land and Bob said nothing when he learned this, betraying no emotion. His relations didn't know what to make of Bob but were struck by the same mysterious quality his grandfather had had, and by Bob's own air of intensity. He was already a public figure, at nineteen one of Jamaica's rising stars, but he was also rumoured to be a gang leader – and they witnessed for themselves his scars and the ratchet in his back pocket.

On Christmas Day 1964 The Wailers played at the Ward Theatre in Kingston: fights broke out as fans battled to get in.

Several people were knifed and controversy raged over The Wailers and the criminals among their following. The band was on the verge of being banned by all major venues in Jamaica when a sensational murder grabbed the headlines, diverting public attention. Jamaica's top dancer had been stabbed to death by her boyfriend, well known trombonist Don Drummond, who worked at Dodd's studio. The killing shocked everyone, especially Bob, who had worked closely with Drummond. By the time The Wailers' single 'Rude Boy' came out in June 1965, discontent among the poor was running higher than ever, with looting and rioting common, and the hopelessness and bitterness felt by many in downtown Kingston was expressed in the song.

In the autumn Cedella wrote inviting Bob to America, and it was decided he should go: he was tired of being manipulated by Dodd, and determined to earn enough to set up his own record label. Bob insisted that he and Rita should get married before he left, and after a brief battle with Rita's aunt, managed to secure her reluctant approval. They were married on 10 February 1966: Rita was nineteen, Bob twenty-one, sporting a short haircut and his black stage suit for the occasion. Like his father before him, he left his wife the day after the wedding.

KING OF REGGAE

Bob didn't take to America: it was too noisy, too 'rush-rush'. He had no work permit, but managed to get work as a waiter, lab assistant and forklift truck driver. He spent his spare time writing songs and refused to have anything to do with local girls who kept ringing up. When Cedella criticized his strange behaviour he tried to explain his ambitions and confessed that he and Rita, his 'queen', were already married. His mother was surprised and disappointed: she had hoped he would make a fresh start in the USA, but it was clear he was intent on returning to Trench Town, and worst of all, he seemed to be becoming interested in Rastafarianism.

In April 1966 Haile Selassie visited Jamaica to be met by a crowd of 100,000. When he left his aeroplane a huge roar went up: tears rolled down his face and he retreated back inside the plane. Later though, as his car passed by, Rita caught a glimpse of the great man – and was convinced she had seen the scars of crucifixion nails on his hands. She wrote to Bob, saying she was likely to become a Rasta.

In October Bob received a letter from the army saying he would soon be called up:

he caught the next plane back to Kingston.
He hadn't yet saved enough to be fully
independent, but with friends' help he
built a stall where he could sell Dodd's
records, plus some on his own new label,
Wail 'N' Soul 'M. Bob noticed that more
and more ghetto youths were becoming
Rastas, and now Rita's experience had
really set him thinking. He talked to Joe
Higgs, who explained the laws and prin-
ciples of the faith. Bunny had already been
a Rasta for years, and in the spring of 1967,
Peter and Bob started growing dreadlocks,
too. The Wailers were the first of the
Jamaican bands to adopt a strictly Rasta
identity: speaking in patois, following a
careful diet, and smoking huge quantities
of herb. They were still recording with
Coxsone, but their output slowed, and
before long they were short of money.

Rita Marley

On stage in Kingston two days after being
shot in the arm

Bob and Rita moved to St Ann, where they farmed, living frugally while Bob concentrated on writing songs.

Peter and Bunny continued to work with Dodd, until a conflict erupted: Dodd ordered them to leave for good and called the police to get rid of them. After this, rumours circulated that the police were after The Wailers. Bunny was busted for possession of herb in 1967 and served a 14-month jail sentence; Bob spent 48 hours behind bars on a set-up traffic offence; and the following year Peter Tosh was jailed after an anti-Rhodesia demonstration

After Bunny's release Bob returned to Kingston. The Wailers got together again and decided to approach Bob's first producer, Leslie Kong, as he seemed the only one prepared to deal with them. Kong's brothers were wary, remembering Bob's eerie prediction years before, but Kong himself dismissed this as superstitious nonsense. He produced a number of songs for them, but The Wailers weren't at home with the trend for rock-steady, and none of the records sold well. It seemed the band had lost their grip on the charts.

At about this time, singer Lee 'Scratch' Perry brought out 'People Funny, Boy': it was an instant hit. It had a new, slow, beat, which was picked up by The Maytals' 'Do The Reggay' in 1968 – and developing from this, reggae became the new sound.

Perry and his band The Upsetters hit the British charts the following year, causing a sensation on tour. When The Upsetters returned to Jamaica The Wailers approached them and Bob persuaded them to break with Perry and to join forces. Perry was livid. He even threatened to kill Bob for poaching his band – but instead the two men agreed to meet. After the meeting they announced that Lee Perry was producer of The Wailers – a new reggae 'supergroup'. Bob and Perry had even co-written 'Small Axe', a song warning the Big T'ree studios in Jamaica that they were a force to be reckoned with. (It was certainly hard to ignore Perry: as a producer he used to plant his artists' records in his garden!)

The new 'supergroup' combined the original Wailers with Upsetters' bassist Aston (Family Man) Barrett and drummer

Carlton Barrett, his brother. Lee Perry worked on the band's style, encouraging Bob to tighten up his singing, and emphasizing The Wailers' 'gutsy' sound. It worked. Their first album, *Soul Rebels*, came out in 1970, and was snapped up by fans who had all but written off The Wailers. It sold well, not just in Jamaica, but to West Indians in Britain, too. Bob bought a car with his share of the proceeds, and there was enough left over to help accommodate his family, which now included baby Cedella and 2-year-old Ziggy.

A second album, *Soul Revolution*, did so well it prompted Leslie Kong to cash in on the band's success. He scraped together a collection of their old rock-steady tracks to be released as *The Best of The Wailers*.

They were outraged, claiming their best
was yet to come, and Kong's brothers
were once again uneasy, remembering
Bob's prediction. Kong himself was happy: unwary Wailers' fans rushed to buy the
Best Of album, and within weeks his
accountant told him he was a millionaire. That day he went home early, feeling ill – and died from a sudden heart
attack.

Since 1968 The Wailers had also been
working with black American singer
Johnny Nash and his promoter Danny
Sims. Then, in 1970, Sims suggested that
Bob join Nash in Sweden to collaborate
on a film score. Bob's input came to
nothing, but instead Sims organized a
Wailers tour of England – which turned
out to mean appearances at schools in the

Midlands. He promised a 'real' tour later, though, and The Wailers agreed to work with Nash on more songs, some of which were extremely successful – for Nash. The Wailers were living in cheap accommodation in London and spent their days rehearsing madly to try and keep warm. Then, out of the blue, Nash and Sims left for Florida. The Wailers were stranded with no money in a wet, cold, alien country.

As a last resort, Bob decided to approach Island Records, a London company set up by white Jamaican Chris Blackwell. For the last few years Blackwell had turned increasingly from Jamaican music to American rock and was by now a millionaire. He still kept in touch with Jamaica, though, and while he knew of The

Bob with his mother, Cedella

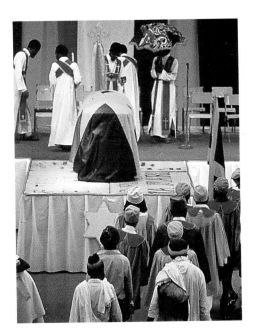

The Rastafarian funeral

Wailers' 'difficult' reputation, he also recognized the only reggae band with enough talent and charisma to make an impact on mainstream pop. He decided to take them on.

The Wailers' morale shot right up. They took their advance and went straight back to Jamaica, where they worked hard to produce an album by the end of the year. Bob then flew to England, only to find himself in the middle of a legal battle: Danny Sims was claiming rights to Bob's music, and so was CBS, which had released an unsuccessful Marley solo single. The Wailers had 'proper' backing now though, and before long Island had negotiated deals – each costing thousands of pounds – which released them from previous contracts.

In early 1973, The Wailers' debut album for Island, *Catch A Fire*, was released to rave reviews in the music press. Roots reggae fans loved it and thousands who had never heard of reggae before rushed out to buy it, too. Chris Blackwell and Bob had worked on it together, substantially revising and remixing tracks to make them more accessible, while the record sleeve, depicting an outsized Zippo lighter, was specially designed to be eye-catching. Next, Blackwell arranged a tour of England and the USA, to capitalise on their success. For part of the tour they were booked to support Sly and the Family Stone, but were swiftly dropped when the crowd showed they preferred The Wailers.

The tour went very well: they had now really started to make a name for themselves outside the Caribbean. Personally, though, it was very different: Bunny decided he couldn't stand the cold, and Joe Higgs flew in to take his place on the tour. Peter, meanwhile, grew increasingly bitter. No longer 'The Wailers', the band was now billed 'Bob Marley and The Wailers': Peter blamed 'Chris Whiteworst' and complained incessantly, though never to Bob's face.

Later in 1973 Island released *Burnin*, complete with pictures of Kingston's shantytowns and a photo of Bob with a huge spliff. The tracks were powerful, especially 'I Shot the Sheriff' (later covered by Eric Clapton) and 'Get Up, Stand Up'.

Suddenly Bob was in all the papers, proclaimed the king of reggae and the Jamaican Mick Jagger. Paul McCartney and Keith Richards became high-profile fans: reggae was the hippest sound around. Bob was now being hailed as a major modern poet, but on the 'Burnin' tour, tensions within the band were growing. They hadn't made much money despite their success, and it seemed Bob was getting all the attention. Then came the English leg of the tour, which was dispiriting: audiences fell off and it was so bitterly cold the band often performed in overcoats. Eventually Bob and Peter came to blows, and the last few dates of the tour were cancelled. By 1974 the original Wailers had unofficially split up.

Crowds of mourners gather for the funeral

The Bob Marley Museum in Kingston

Bob spent much of that year in the studio, working on a new LP, *Knotty Dread*, which to Bob's horror was released as *Natty Dread*, completely obscuring the concept of a wild, natural Rastaman. Tracks included 'Rebel Music' and 'Revolution', songs whose lyrics greatly disturbed the authorities in Jamaica. Jamaica Radio refused to play one of these tracks, until Bob – and a friend, armed with a baseball bat – threatened the DJs. After that it was number 1 in Jamaica all summer, but while Bob was off touring Europe and the USA again, the Jamaican police publicly beat up Peter Tosh, apparently to make an example of him.

Unaware of trouble at home, Bob Marley and The Wailers were making a huge impact: the crowds loved them. With

Bunny and Peter gone, harmonies were now supplied by the I-Threes, a female trio composed of Rita Marley, Marcia Griffiths and Judy Mowatt, which lent a new dimension to the songs. In July 1975, one of the band's London Lyceum shows was recorded for a live album, and this caused a sensation – especially the haunting 'No Woman, No Cry', drawn straight from ghetto life.

The *Live!* album was released only in Europe to start with, but Island soon recognized it would be a hit in the USA, too. The band had even started to get airplay on white American rock stations, and Bob himself was now a fully-fledged star, widely quoted on politics, religion and personal philosophy as well as music. He seemed to enjoy interviews, taking his time with reporters and answering questions he didn't like with his thoughts on Haile Selassie, or with sarcastic questions of his own.

'Me not of this world, y'know,' he claimed in one interview around this time. 'Me live in the world, but I'm not of the world.' Such oblique comments no doubt helped sustain his mystique, as did his often contradictory statements – or fantasies: he liked to tell journalists that he wasn't married and that his mother lived in Africa! He was clear enough on reggae though, which he called King Music: 'You getting a three-in-one music. You getting a happy rhythm with a sad sound with a good vibration . . . it's roots music.'

Bob's success continued: by 1976 he had replaced Stevie Wonder as the Third World's greatest musical superstar. The same year saw the release of *Rastaman Vibration* (with an embossed cover announcing 'This album jacket is great for cleaning herb'), and though some hard-core reggae fans were disappointed, it was a huge success. A three-month tour behind the album began in Philadelphia and fans were surprised by the subdued and mellow performance of their hero: they weren't to know his mother was in the audience! Album after album followed, each a best-seller, and Bob found himself a living legend, repeatedly touring the world and playing to sell-out crowds.

HOPE ROAD

In the early 1970s Chris Blackwell had bought a large, shabby house in Hope Road, a smart area of Kingston. Island House was to be his new Jamaican base, but his new star took a liking to it, and he decided Bob could take it over. Gossip spread through Trench Town that Bob was living in a mansion, but no-one believed it – until they saw it for themselves. Bob told the downtown 'dreads' they were welcome at Hope Road, but they were sceptical about this: it was a long way from the ghetto, and the house seemed full of Bob's rich new friends.

As Bob's success grew, so, it seemed, did the crowd around him. Rita and the family were there, Bunny, and the frequently-changing members of The Wailers' band, though Peter Tosh now visited only occasionally. Other Hope Road regulars included visiting shantytown Rastas, Antonio 'Gilly' Gilbert (Bob's 'ital' cook), Alan 'Skill' Cole (professional footballer and now a close friend of Bob's), Neville Garrick (resident designer), Diane Jobson (Bob's lawyer), 'Sticko' Mitchell (secretary) and Lips (Bob's bodyguard). There was also a constant stream of women, foremost among whom were Jamaican actress

Esther Anderson and the model Cindy Breakspeare, later Miss World.

Hope Road was like a commune, with lots of herb, music, casual sex, and children running in and out. Bob and Rita now had another child, but as Bob once said, he wanted to have 'as many children as dere were shells on de beach'. He achieved a total of ten (legally recognized) offspring by various women, and it was rumoured there were many more. This, though, was not particularly unusual by Jamaican standards: Toddy Livingston, for instance, fathered sixteen by a number of different women. Bob made no secret of his liaisons, and Rita seemed to take them in her stride. Bob himself joked that if a child had a lop-sided way of speaking, then he knew it was one of his.

Life followed a familiar pattern at Hope Road. Bob, a serious Rasta, was committed to a healthy lifestyle, and each day began at sunrise with him and several of the regulars setting off for a jog. Sometimes, on Sundays, they ran to Port Royal Point, eighteen miles away. They often went to the beach, or to the Cane River Falls where they would wash each others' dreadlocks, and then on to the market to buy food. If there was no rehearsing, or recording, everyone hung around until it was time for the afternoon football game. When they were working, it was intensive, with Bob tireless and very exacting in rehearsals. Evenings were invariably spent singing, smoking herb and discussing Rasta ideas.

Bob had slipped happily into the role of superstar: previous nicknames had included 'Five Foot Four', but now he was 'Skipper' – or 'Tuff Gong' as he used to be known in Trench Town. At Hope Road, speakers blared out reggae at all hours deliberately to annoy the neighbours. Bob bought a silver BMW, and when challenged on this by downtown dreads, justified it by saying BMW stood for Bob Marley and The Wailers!

In June 1976, Jamaica's governor-general declared a state of emergency, putting the island under martial law. It was the lead-up to an election, and there had been a spate of violence – most parents had even withdrawn their children from school until after the election, on 16 December. Bob was approached to do an outdoor concert, 'Smile Jamaica', on 5 December. He was assured it was not political, just a concert to help keep the peace, so he agreed.

A week before the concert there was a general atmosphere of unrest, and armed guards arrived at Hope Road to give 24-hour protection. Then one evening, a few days later, someone noticed the guards were missing: at the same time shots rang out. Bob was in the kitchen with Don Taylor, his personal manager, and Don, chatting as he crossed the room, caught the bullets intended for Bob. Rita was shot in the head as she ran out with the children, then another gunman fired wildly into the kitchen: only one bullet hit Bob, tearing into his arm.

The attackers escaped. It was amazing that no-one was killed. The injured were rushed to hospital, stunned and terrified; two were in a critical state and Rita needed surgery to remove a bullet from her scalp. After Bob was treated a police escort whisked him away to a camp in the mountains. It is not clear what the attack was about: most assumed it was political, but others, maintaining Bob was mixed up in the Jamaican underworld, said it was an act of vengeance. Bob himself said it was probably jealousy of his success – but he was very upset, and of course no-one knew if the would-be assassins would strike again.

The day of the concert arrived, and Bob didn't know whether to go ahead. Neither Bunny nor Peter Tosh, now both solo artists, had turned up for their scheduled slots. Other musicians had stepped in, though, and a crowd of 50,000 had already gathered. Bravely, Bob decided to go ahead and sent someone to round up the rest of the band.

The stage was fully exposed to any sniper. When Bob ran on there were massive cheers. Bob stepped up to the micro-phone: 'When me decided to do dis yere concert, me was told dere was no politics. I just wanted ta play fe da love of da people!' The atmosphere was highly charged, but no attack came and after an impassioned ninety minutes, Bob wound up with a dramatic dance, acting out the shooting. The drama was heightened by Rita: with no time to change she had come to the concert in her night-dress, a scarf wound round her bandages.

After the concert Bob lay low for a while. He went to America and then to Britain, where he and the Wailers cut twenty new songs during the winter of 1977. Half of these were for the explosive *Exodus* album, released that spring, the others, mostly love songs and dance tracks, for *Kaya*. This came out the following year and was received with surprise and some criticism, which Bob shrugged off impatiently, tellling those who accused him of abandoning his protests that he refused to sing the same songs for ever.

Bob did not go back to Jamaica until spring 1978. The island was now in even greater political turmoil, perhaps on the brink of civil war, or a military coup, and Bob had been approached in London about playing at the 'One Love' Peace

Concert. It was being organized by Jamaica's two rival political parties, forced uneasily together in a panicky attempt to soothe the public. The 'One Love' Concert was a telling measure of Bob Marley's stature: not only did he play, sensationally, but he somehow persuaded the warring political leaders, two bitter enemies, to come on stage and lock hands with his.

The success of that concert seemed to give Bob a new burst of energy and he threw himself into a world tour that took in America, Europe, Australia and Japan. That year too, he went to Africa for the first time, and was shocked to find the same poverty and corruption so familiar at home. He was buoyed up, though, by his later experience in Zimbabwe. He had been deeply honoured to be invited to play at the official Zimbabwe Independence Day ceremony in 1980, celebrating the passing of Rhodesia and the end of white colonial rule. Bob was triumphant – Zimbabwe was one of the high points of his life.

All was not well, though. Bob was losing weight and had begun to look ill. The problem had started some years earlier, in 1977, when he had injured a toe playing football: the toenail had been wrenched off and the wound refused to heal. A specialist who examined Bob's foot had detected cancer cells and advised Bob to have the toe amputated as soon as possible to stop the cancer spreading. Bob refused: 'I and I don't allow a mon to be dismantled!' He knew the risks, but as a

Rasta, saw his body as a temple – and decided to let nature take its course. So the toe remained, but by 1980 it had become ulcerated and very painful, though most of the band were unaware of this.

In September 1980, Bob and the Wailers set off for the 'Uprising' tour of the USA. The band knew something was wrong when they reached New York. For years they had all shared the same hotels: now, suddenly, Bob was in a hotel 40 blocks away.

One morning he went out jogging with Skill Cole. They were running through Central Park when suddenly Bob collapsed; he could hardly move. He seemed to recover after a few hours but his doctor took him to see a neurologist. The diagnosis was bad. His collapse had been a stroke, he had a cancerous brain tumour, and maybe only two weeks left to live.

Bob was stunned, but flew to Pittsburgh and insisted on playing the following night. It was his last ever gig. Further tests revealed cancer of the lungs and stomach, and as his illness got worse, arguments raged over whether to keep his condition secret. Then the doctors began chemotherapy and his dreadlocks fell out. Bob was in agony. As a last resort his family sent him to Germany, to a controversial cancer specialist. Here Bob struggled on for a further six months. In the end he weighed less than six stone and could hardly even hold his guitar. Finally, on 11 May 1981, Bob died on his way back to Jamaica. He was thirty-six.

Jamaica declared a national day of mourning. Bob's body was flown home and 40,000 Jamaicans filed past to pay their last respects. He had been awarded the Jamaican Order of Merit, and a banner proclaiming 'The Hon. Robert Nesta Marley OM' was proudly displayed among Ethiopian flags and portraits of both Bob and Haile Selassie. After the funeral service, his coffin was driven slowly back to St. Ann, along roads lined with mourners, to the hill where he was born.

Bob Marley was an extraordinary character, a powerful but elusive figure hailed by many after his death as a prophet or Christ figure. Bob himself certainly knew he was a great musician: 'My music will go on forever', he said. 'Maybe it's a fool say that, but when me know facts me can say facts. My music go on forever.'